Kings Mountain Walking Tour Guide

by

Robert M. Dunkerly

DORRANCE PUBLISHING CO., INC
PITTSBURGH, PENNSYLVANIA 15222

ISBN #0-8059-6117-8
Printed in the United States of America

First Printing

For information or to order additional books, please write:
Dorrance Publishing Co., Inc.
701 Smithfield Street
Third Floor
Pittsburgh, Pennsylvania 15222
U.S.A.
1-800-788-7654
Or visit or web site and on-line catalog at
www.dorrancepublishing.com

Contents

Maps

Introduction

This guide uses the latest historical and archaeological research available to provide insight into the battle of Kings Mountain as one walks the battlefield trail. Also included is information on the monuments, the history of the park, and an overview of the campaign in the south. The interpretation of events, along with any mistakes, are my own.

Kings Mountain remains a relatively unknown battle to most Americans in the twenty-first century. This is ironic since most of the American Revolution's southern battles are protected as national or state parks, while the larger and more famous battlefields of the north are chiefly gone. Most Americans today think of the Revolution as a northern or New England phenomenon. The war did begin in the north and the largest battles were fought there, but few of those sites are preserved today. Long Island, White Plains, Germantown, Trenton, Harlem Heights, and most of Brandywine have all been lost to urban growth or lie unprotected. Today one may visit every major southern battle site from Moores Creek to Yorktown. The battlefield tourist visiting the Carolinas is fortunate indeed.

Kings Mountain, in the words of President Herbert Hoover in 1930, is a place of "inspiring memories." It was not only one of the most decisive American victories of the war, it was also one of the more unique battles of the Revolution in many aspects. Kings Mountain came after a string of devastating American defeats, turning the tide, in the words of Thomas Jefferson. It was also one of the few battles of the war fought between Americans: There were no English troops involved. The American or patriot forces who came here were all militia volunteers; there were no Continental soldiers among them. Facing them were an equal number of American Loyalists fighting for the crown. Kings Mountain was also one of the few battles won by the rifle, an unheard of occurrence during the war.

The rifle would not figure so prominently in any other engagement. Another unique characteristic of the battle is that it was also fought on steep, wooded slopes, unlike the open fields of most encounters. In terms of troops, terrain, and weapons, Kings Mountain stands alone in the course of the war.

I would like to thank the following for their assistance and constructive criticism: Chief Ranger Chris Revels of Kings Mountain National Military Park and Research Assistant Heather South with the York County Historical Center.

A word about sources:

Reconstructing the events that unfolded here on October 7, 1780, was no easy task. Unlike today's military, the Continental army did not file official after-action reports. Very few battle accounts exist, most of them written by officers, thereby excluding the experiences of the rank and file. There are also more American than Loyalist accounts, again slanting the available information. Pension applications are also useful sources about the battle, but are limited in number and vary greatly in content.

Lyman C. Draper's, *Kings Mountain and Its Heroes*, published in 1880, is by far the best study of the battle. Draper thoroughly researched his topic and corresponded with descendants of the Kings Mountain soldiers and local residents of the area. He pieced together a decidedly romanticized and one-sided but definitely complete story of the battle. More recently, Dr. Bobby Moss's research into the participants has shed light on other accounts, however our sources on the battle remain limited. Despite its shortcomings, I have heavily relied on Draper since it is the closest thing we have to a primary source.

A note on names:

To avoid confusion I will refer to the two sides at Kings Mountain as the Loyalists and the Americans, even though both were American born. The terms Tory and Rebel have derogatory connotations and I have tried to avoid their use. When I refer to the American riflemen, I am talking about Campbell's American army; the Loyalists are Ferguson's troops. Recent debate has questioned the traditional terms of Loyalist and Patriot, since in a sense both groups were loyal to a cause and patriotic in their own ways. As throughout history, winners write the books, and over two hundred years of Revolutionary history refers to the Americans as Patriots.

Background

After five years of indecisive fighting in the northern colonies, the Revolutionary War was stalemated. General George Washington's Continental army faced the British army under General Henry Clinton outside of New York City, but not for long. France had entered the war, and British troops were needed on other fronts. Losing the North American colonies would be bad; the loss of Gibraltar, India, or the West Indies a disaster.

As the English reoriented for a worldwide strategy, they developed a solution for the American Rebellion: conquer the south. This region had been relatively untouched thus far, and it was felt that many Loyalists here would rise to support the Crown. With the Americans divided, they would be easier to conquer. Using a small core of British regulars, they would be augmented by local Loyalists, armed and trained by the British army. After securing an area the British troops could then move on, leaving the Loyalists in control. English forces captured Savannah in December 1778 and in one blow took Georgia out of the war. The next year preparations were made for taking South Carolina.

In May of 1780, the English captured Charleston, taking over five thousand American prisoners. This was the worst defeat in American military history until the fall of Bataan in the Philippines in 1942. From Charleston, British forces spread across South Carolina, establishing control. In August a second American army met disaster at Camden. The remnants of the Continental army fled to North Carolina, leaving the southern colony in British hands.

The English plan seemed to be working perfectly. To organize Loyalists, the English turned to Major Patrick Ferguson, a talented young officer. Throughout the summer of 1780, Ferguson recruited, armed, and drilled

1

several thousand Carolina Loyalists. He issued a proclamation that the Americans must stop resisting British authority or face destruction "with fire and sword." The prospect of English troops invading the piedmont and mountain settlements galvanized the American militia.

Colonel Isaac Shelby of North Carolina began to organize militia of the overmountain or backwater settlements. Shelby hoped to unite militia from the Carolina piedmont with his overmountain frontiersmen to meet Ferguson. The overmountain men came from today's east Tennessee. These predominately Scotch-Irish settlers were fiercely independent and feared the British threat. On their own initiative and without official sanction, militia from five states (Virginia, the two Carolinas, Georgia, and modern Tennessee) organized to meet Ferguson. Their march has become legendary.

The American militia rendezvoused at Sycamore Shoals (modern Elizabeth, Tennessee) on September 25, 1780. They began to march east, over the mountains, and were joined by other commands as they went. Today their route is commemorated by the Overmountain Victory National Historic Trail, which preserves sites along the march, holds special events, and preserves the memory of the Revolution in the Carolinas.

One of their stops was at Quaker Meadows, (Morganton, North Carolina). Owned by the brothers Colonel Charles and Major Joseph McDowell, the troops rested and were treated to the McDowells' beef cattle. Here Winston and Cleveland's men joined the army. Moving further south they came to Gilbert Town, near modern Rutherfordton. Ferguson had just recently left the area.

As the Americans moved south, a different officer took turns commanding each day. Such an arrangement would not work once they neared the enemy, so at Gilbert Town Shelby proposed that Campbell be appointed overall commander: his men had come the farthest, and he was the only officer not from the Carolinas.

When they neared the Carolina border, Colonel James Williams of South Carolina arrived to tell the command that Ferguson had withdrawn to Ninety Six. Actually the Loyalists were near the Broad River, marching toward Kings Mountain. Williams hoped to use the assembled force in a strike against the large British base to the south and enhance his reputation. The next day, however, Colonel William Hill rode in to reveal the true location of Ferguson.

On October 6 the South Carolinians under Williams, Lacy, Hill, and Hawthrone met the rest of the army at Hannah's Cowpens, a clearing about thirty miles from Kings Mountain. Deciding he must strike before Ferguson got away, Campbell chose nine hundred of the best men to march on to Kings Mountain that night.

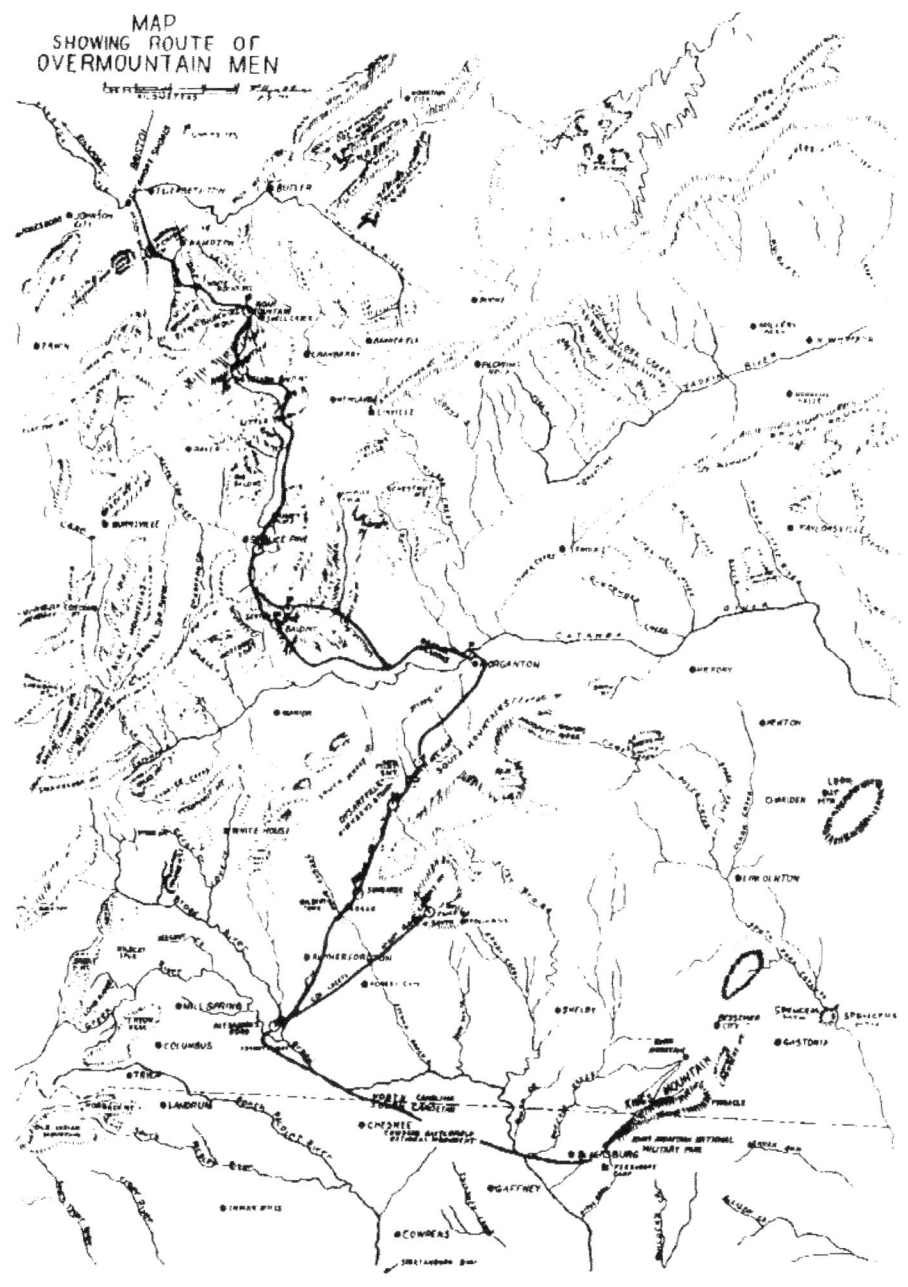

Map 1. The March to Kings Mountain

Map from Pat Alderman's <u>One Heroic Hour at Kings Mountain</u>

Weapons

An understanding of flintlock weapons is critical to the Kings Mountain story. The military weapon of the day was the smoothbore musket. Muskets, both the English Brown Bess and French Charleville, had an effective range of about one hundred yards. Highly inaccurate, their advantage lay in speed. A trained soldier could load and fire it four times a minute. The musket was a mass-produced weapon, its parts were interchangeable, and it fired a standard sized ball. Musket stocks were thick and reinforced with metal plates, so if necessary they could be used as clubs. The most important aspect of a musket was the socket bayonet, which still allowed the soldier to load and fire since it did not block the muzzle. British troops were well drilled with the bayonet. Bayonet charges won or lost battles during the Revolution.

The inaccuracy of the musket influenced the tactics of the eighteenth century battlefield. An officer used the regiment as his weapon, not the individual soldiers. A massed volley sent a stream of lead at the enemy and followed by a bayonet charge could rout an opposing line. Shock was used to break the enemy's line. Linear combat followed a steady pace of volleying, loading, volleying, and a bayonet charge.

The rifle was a hunting weapon, and contrary to popular belief its military use was very limited. Families on the frontier used the rifle for protection and to put food on their tables. In times of warfare, rifles were pressed into service by the militia. With grooves cut down the length of the barrel, rifles sent the ball straighter and farther than a smoothbore musket. Riflemen could hit targets 200 to 400 yards away, depending on circumstances. Their disadvantages, however, were many.

A rifle took nearly a full minute to load, since powder had to be measured from a horn and the charge took longer to ram down the rifled barrel. Rifles were also individually made by gunsmiths, so supplying a group of riflemen who needed various spare parts and calibres of ammunition was difficult. Rifles were also delicate; their stocks were thin and light and could not be used as a club in close combat. Nor did rifles take bayonets. In open field combat riflemen were helpless in the face of a bayonet charge.

Riflemen fired individually, each loading at their own pace. Thus riflemen could keep a steady rolling fire going, whereas musket-bearing troops followed the pattern outlined above. In the combat that flowed up and down the ridges of Kings Mountain, a certain degree of flexible leadership and control was demanded. The American riflemen had to retreat, but not too far. Judging when to stand their ground or retire to reload was a skill learned in clashes with Indians and Loyalists on the frontier.

With that said, bear in mind that some of the Loyalists had rifles, and no doubt many of the American militia had muskets. As a general rule, however, Ferguson's troops had drilled all summer with muskets, and the American militia opposing them were armed largely with rifles. Neither weapon could be loaded while sitting, kneeling, or lying down. Both had their advantages and limitations, and each represented a specific fighting style.

Commanders

American

The American or Patriot forces were led by Colonel William Campbell of Virginia. Campbell headed a group of various militia commands from several states and departments, and their mutual cooperation at Kings Mountain is one of the neglected success stories of the campaign. Rival officers do not always work well together, even in the face of a common enemy, and the cooperation exhibited on the route to Kings Mountain was remarkable indeed.

Isaac Shelby was the first to organize a response to Ferguson's army. Shelby had been in the field for some time battling the Loyalists in the upcountry of South Carolina, and after the American defeat at Camden he withdrew to the overmountain settlements in search of help. He appealed to Campbell and John Sevier, who both responded with troops and supplies.

Campbell had served in the 1st Virginia Regiment in the early days of the war. He then spent several years in southwestern Virginia, battling Loyalists and Indians. He was well qualified to lead the expedition. Campbell later led his Virginia riflemen to the Battle of Guilford Courthouse. He married Elizabeth Henry, the sister of Patrick Henry. He would probably be better known today had he not died of disease just weeks before the surrender of Yorktown.

Shelby and Sevier are best known for their post-war careers. Both men were well-respected frontier leaders who helped battle the Cherokee in East Tennessee. Sevier would become the first governor of Tennessee; Shelby would be Kentucky's.

Benjamin Cleveland established a reputation as a tough militia leader who fought throughout the war in the Carolina piedmont. Joseph Winston would command North Carolina militia again at Guilford Courthouse, five months later. Many towns, communities, and counties across the Carolinas, Tennessee, and the Deep South are named in honor of these North Carolina men.

The South Carolinians under colonels Williams, Hill, Lacy, and Hawthorne had been in the field since the spring, mostly acting in small partisan groups fighting the Loyalists. These troops were usually led by Thomas Sumter, but he had gone to meet with the governor of South Carolina regarding a command controversy with Williams.

One last point about the American army—it was heterogeneous force. While each unit came from a specific region, research reveals that there was considerable movement among American soldiers during 1780, and membership in units was fluid. As the English took over much of South Carolina, many from the Palmetto state fled to join militia in North Carolina. The same is true of Georgians. While a unit may have been raised from one region, there were a number of refugees found in each battalion. Williams, for example, had many North Carolinians under his command, and McDowell had some South Carolinians with him.

Loyalist

Major Patrick Ferguson was the famous but somewhat romanticized head of the Loyalist troops at Kings Mountain. After joining the British army at age fifteen, Ferguson rose rapidly and showed great promise. He served in several European campaigns before the outbreak of the American rebellion.

Ferguson is best remembered for inventing a breechloading rifle, which actually improved on a design already in use. The weapon, a rifled version of the Brown Bess, could be loaded by unscrewing the trigger guard and exposing a hole at the barrel's breech. He demonstrated his invention before the king and other military commanders, who received it favorably. At the battle of Brandywine, Pennsylvania, in 1777, Ferguson had command of a one hundred man corps armed with Ferguson Rifles. They performed well, but he was injured in the battle. While recovering his men were redistributed to their former regiments and the Ferguson Rifles put in storage.

Ferguson's actions at Brandywine indicate something of his character. He was scouting ahead of the army when he spied an American officer in the distance. Ferguson could have easily hit him, but such an act was against the accepted rules of warfare at the time. European armies did not target officers, and Ferguson strictly followed this code. Later Ferguson learned that it was George Washington that he had within his sights that day.

By 1780 he had recovered and joined the British invasion of the South. Having lost the use of his right arm at Brandywine, he taught himself to write, fence, and use a sword with his left. He also adopted the use of a whistle to command troops. Cornwallis sent Ferguson into the backcountry to recruit Loyalist militia, and the choice seemed perfect. He developed a reputation for fairness and honesty when dealing with Americans and opposed brutal tactics to control the population.

His death at Kings Mountain was a severe blow to the English army. With his death also ended attempts to further promote the Ferguson Rifle. Historians and reenactors debate its merits and shortcomings to this day. Whether any were used here in this battle is uncertain; there may have been a few among officers or sharpshooters, yet it is clear that most of his troops were armed with muskets.

Captain Abraham DePeyster of the American Volunteers served as Ferguson's second in command and would surrender the army after Ferguson's death. Descended from an aristocratic Dutch New York family, he was paroled to Charleston and moved to New Brunswick after the war.

Lieutenant Anthony Alliare commanded the American Volunteers during the battle. A fellow New Yorker, he escaped from Betharbara, North Carolina, and made his way back to British lines in South Carolina. After the war he also moved to New Brunswick and died in 1838.

Major Daniel Plummer led the Fair Forest Militia, one of the largest militia units present here. Wounded and left for dead on the battlefield, he later fought at Ninety Six in 1781. After the war Plummer left for Florida.

Major Patrick Cunningham commanded the Little River Militia, the other large militia regiment here. Like many others, he escaped capture and later fought again at Ninety Six.

Ambrose Mills, from the Green River area of North Carolina, led a group of his neighbors from that region. With a reputation as a bandit and thief, Mills was executed at Bickerstaff's plantation after the battle.

The Loyalist army consisted of about 1100 men. On the morning of the battle, Ferguson sent about 200 men out on a scouting expedition, the only troops not captured that day. He had about one hundred men of the American Volunteers, Provincial Regulars from the New York City area. The rest of his troops were Carolina militia. As with the Americans, men from both Carolinas enlisted in these South Carolina units.

The Battlefield

Although the terrain has changed little in over two hundred years, the vegetation is completely unlike that encountered by the armies. At the time of the battle an old growth forest of large trees covered these slopes. While the hillsides were wooded, the crest of the ridge was treeless, as it is today. A road ran through the area, part of which will be seen on the walking trail. Both armies approached the ridge from the west on this road. Several springs are located at the base of the hill, and they provided water for both sides in the aftermath of the fighting.

The US military uses a mnemonic known as KOCOA to analyze battlefield terrain, which is useful in understanding the battle here at Kings Mountain. The elements of this include Key terrain, Obstacles, Cover and concealment, Observations and fields of fire, and Avenues of approach and retreat. As you walk the trail, observe the terrain and keep these factors in mind, for they influenced the fighting on these wooded slopes.

Tour

Begin in the visitor center with the film and exhibits. The park brochure has an excellent map which will complement this walking tour. The tour stops are designed to accompany the waysides and monuments along the trail.

On October 7, 1780, Ferguson's army was camped on Kings Mountain, having taken position there the day before. Ferguson felt confident in its steep slopes and in his men's training; he ordered no fortifications built, nor did he continue on to Charlotte and the main British army. He knew the Americans were coming and chose to stand his ground and fight here. Ferguson obviously underestimated his enemy and overestimated his troop's capabilities given the terrain. Why he chose to fight here remains a mystery, but his last letter sheds light on his thinking. In a dispatch sent out that morning, Ferguson wrote that he was on Kings Mountain, and he was king of that mountain, and God Almighty could not drive him from it. His last letter expresses confidence in his position and asks General Lord Cornwallis for reinforcements.

The American forces had split up at Cowpens the evening of the sixth. Knowing Ferguson was within marching distance of Charlotte, Campbell hoped to catch him before he escaped or received reinforcements. Nine hundred of the best men were chosen and marched all night toward Kings Mountain. The remainder were to follow the next day at their own pace.

A steady rain fell that night, forcing the men to use blankets and hunting shirts to keep their rifles and powder dry. The army forded the Broad River at Cherokee Ford and paused for a quick meal. Most had little food. As the army neared Kings Mountain they encountered local civilians who knew where the Loyalist camp was. Major Chronicle and Captain Mattocks of present-day Gaston County knew firsthand of Ferguson's position, since they had used the site for a deer hunting camp the year before.

Within a few miles the army encountered a girl who had taken some chickens to Ferguson's camp that morning. Next a messenger was taken, and Ferguson's last letter to Cornwallis fell into American hands. The boy also said that Ferguson was wearing a red and white checkered duster. By about 3 P.M. the rain stopped, and the Americans neared Kings Mountain. About one quarter mile from the ridge the Americans split up, leaving their horses under a small guard. The various forces divided to surround the ridge. At this point Campbell moved out with his Virginia militia, and each commander acted independently. The wide area of the battlefield prevented Campbell from exercising direct control as the battle unfolded. (Refer to the map for troop positions.)

Bear in mind that it had rained all night, and the Americans had ridden over thirty miles with one short break. Adrenaline probably kicked in as the men grappled with lack of sleep and food. U.S. Army research shows that troops who have a hot meal will perform much better in combat, but that option was not available here. It was early October, so it was probably damp and somewhat cool that afternoon. In humid, damp weather black powder is often unreliable, and thick clouds of smoke will hang in the woods, obscuring visibility. Slick rocks and wet leaves also retarded the movement of soldiers as they advanced.

This account from Virginian Benjamin Sharp relates the approach to Kings Mountain: We "fell in with three men who informed us that they were just from the British camp, that they were posted on King's Mountain, and that there was a picket guard on the road not far ahead of us. These men were detained lest they should find means to inform the enemy of our approach, and Colonel Shelby, with a select party, undertook to surprise the picket; this he accomplished without firing a gun or giving the least alarm, and it was hailed by the army as a good omen. We then moved on, and as we approached the mountain, the roll of British drums informed us that we had something to do."

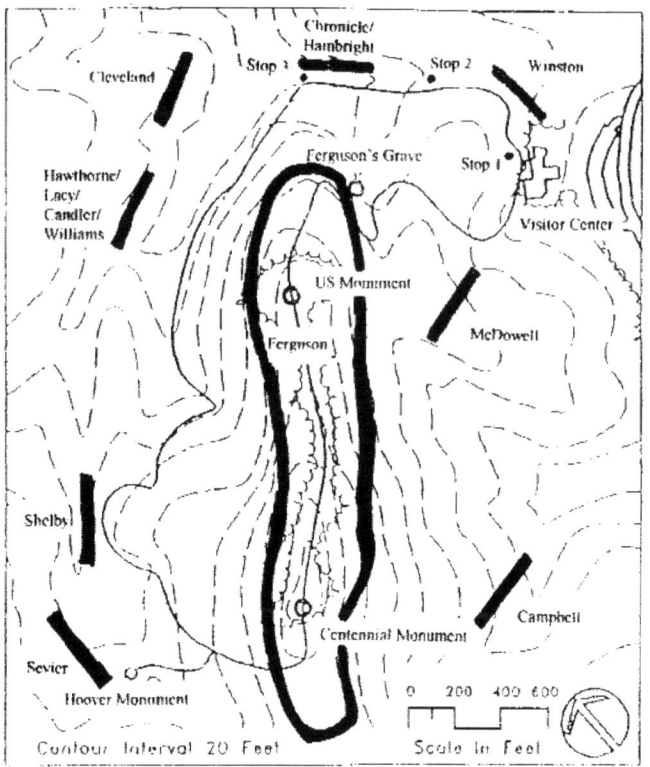

Map 2. Stops 1-3

Stop 1: Behind Visitor Center: Winston's Attack
After exiting the Visitor Center, pause on the back patio to read the way-sides there. Refer to the map while reading the explanation below.

Kings Mountain ridge and the campsite of Ferguson's army lies to your left front. From this area Major Joseph Winston's troops attacked. These troops came from Surry County, North Carolina. Winston's column had gotten separated while taking position and initially assaulted the wrong hill. On finding no enemy troops they continued on and joined the engagement as intended. Winston had about sixty men under arms that afternoon; his losses are unknown.

Winston, along with the neighboring columns led by McDowell and Chronicle, held critical sections of the line. Here they blocked Ferguson's route of retreat to Charlotte. If the Loyalists attempted to get away it would be through this area, so these troops had to hold their ground. As they worked their way up to the crest, Winston's men probably caught glimpses of the tents, wagons, and horses in the Loyalist camp above them.

Stop 2: Fighting in a Forest Primeval
Proceed along the trail and stop at the marker titled "Fighting in a Forest Primeval."

The woods surrounding you today bear little resemblance to the forest that stood here in 1780. This engagement was fought in a climax forest, one of the features that make Kings Mountain a unique Revolutionary War battle. Trees three to four feet thick stood here, reaching one hundred feet into the air. The thick canopy overhead prevented much sunlight from reaching the ground. Consequently there was little undergrowth between the trees. The trees were thicker than today, but widely scattered. Soldiers spoke of moving easily between the trees and using them for cover. Targets could be seen at long distances.

As the area was settled in the nineteenth century, these woods were cleared. The last time was in 1930 to accommodate crowds for President Hoover's visit. The trees you see today have grown back since that time. In 2000 the park began a prescribed burning program in an effort to restore the original battlefield landscape. Controlled burning removes the non-historic underbrush, enriches soils, and removes fuel buildup from contributing to wildfires. Along with the planting of native grasses and the removal of non-native plants, these efforts intend to restore historic views and vistas to the battlefield. Cowpens, Monmouth, Gettysburg, Antietam, and other battle sites are undertaking similar projects.

This is important since to understand the decisions commanders made, we must see what they saw. An appreciation for the terrain that troops faced allows us to understand those factors that helped or retarded their movements and actions.

Stop 3: Chronicle Markers
Continue along the trail, down the slope, and stop in front of the two Chronicle Markers to your right.

Here stand three markers to Major William Chronicle, who fell in this area at the head of his men. He had just shouted his command to "Face the hill!" Chronicle led about twenty South Fork Troops, coming from today's Lincoln and Gaston Counties of North Carolina. They attacked from the hill behind the twin markers, across the roadbed, and up the hill behind you.

Lieutenant Colonel Frederick Hambright took over for Chronicle after he was hit. A German immigrant, Hambright urged his men on in broken English. He was wounded farther up the hill, as will be explained later.

Visible here is also a trace of the original roadbed. This was used by both armies to reach Kings Mountain. The road originally ran straight through the park and was replaced by the modern SC 216. About one quarter mile to the west, on the ridge opposite Ferguson's position, is the site where the American riflemen split up to encircle the mountain. An account by Joseph

Graham relates that when the army reached the opposite ridge, Ferguson's camp "was in full view, about one hundred poles in front." Again, park efforts to restore the old growth forest will allow future visitors to appreciate this lost view.

The older Chronicle Marker on the left has been replaced by the newer marker to the right. The Chronicle Marker, somewhat unimpressive today, holds national significance as one of the oldest Revolutionary War markers in the country. The stone was dedicated in 1815, just thirty-five years after the battle, and some of Chronicle's soldiers were present that day. Despite its gravestone-like appearance, archaeological testing has revealed no burials here at this marker. Chronicle's detachment lost at least thirteen of their twenty men here.

Private James Collins recalled that, "We were soon in motion, every man throwing four or five balls into his mouth to prevent thirst, also to be in readiness to reload quick. The shot of the enemy soon began to pass over us like hail. We soon attempted to climb the hill, but were fiercely charged upon and forced back to our first position; we tried a second time, but met the same fate. . . ." At the close of the fighting he explained that "Their great elevation above us had proved their ruin; they overshot us altogether."

On the slope in front of you, sixteen-year-old Robert Henry was cocking his rifle as a Loyalist closed in. The Loyalist's bayonet skidded down the length of Henry's barrel, passing through his hand and into his thigh. Henry instantly shot and killed his attacker, but the bayonet and musket were stuck in his leg. A fellow soldier had to kick it loose for him. This is one example of the close combat that occurred all along the ridge.

Nearby, William Twitty observed accurate fire from behind a tree on the hilltop. As soon as a head appeared he fired. After the action ceased Twitty retraced his steps to that tree and found one of his neighbors dead on the ground. Similar stories abound.

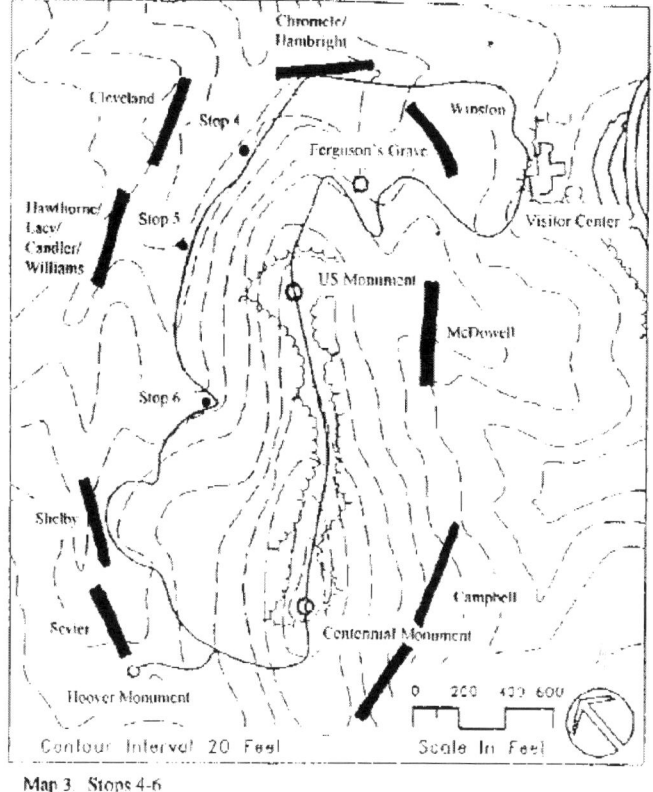

Map 3 Stops 4-6

Stop 4: Cleveland's Attack

*Continue to the marker "Hold Your Place as Ordered." Note the steep slope
in this area to your left, which probably impeded Cleveland's men.*

Colonel Benjamin Cleveland of North Carolina was well known for his bitter hatred of Loyalists during the Revolution. In this vicinity he led about one hundred-ten troops from Wilkes County into battle. Cleveland lost at least fourteen men in his attack, including the three Lewis brothers, who were all wounded here.

Cleveland's regiment was one of the last to fall into line, having been delayed by swampy ground after leaving the road. No doubt their progress was retarded by low ground saturated from the previous evening's rain. To inspire his men he roared, "My brave fellows, we have beaten the Tories and we can beat them again. They are all cowards: if they had the spirit of men, they would join with their fellow citizens in supporting the independence of their country." This is one example of the inspiring speeches that each commander gave to his troops.

Stop 5: South Carolina and Georgia Troops
The next stop is the marker titled, "Shoot Tree to Tree."

Although the battle took place in South Carolina (you are currently about one and one half miles below the state line), most of the troops who fought here were from North Carolina. The South Carolina contingent came from various commands, some of Thomas Sumter's troops, as well as militia from Union, York, and Chester Counties. A group also came under the leadership of Colonel James Williams from Chester, Union, and York Counties in South Carolina as well as Lincoln and Cleveland Counties in North Carolina.

In the days before catching up to Ferguson, Williams had claimed credit for the American victory at Musgrove Mill. He also attempted to steer the troops under Campbell away from Kings Mountain, hoping to attack Ninety Six. For these reasons Williams's followers shrank and he acted independently in the battle. The true nature of the feuding between Sumter and Williams remains clouded to this day. The remainder of the South Carolinians were led by colonels Edward Lacy and James Hawthorne. Colonel William Hill, recovering from a wound at the battle of Hanging Rock, remained behind at Cowpens, no doubt disappointed to miss what would be one of the most important battles of the war. There were probably no more than seventy South Carolinians total.

Augmenting this small force was a contingent of thirty Georgians under Major William Candler. Georgia had fallen to the English in 1779 and the militia who fled joined up with the Overmountain Men to attack Ferguson. The South Carolinians lost about fifteen men in the battle, the Georgians at least one.

Toward the close of the action Colonel Williams was hit and mortally wounded. Although unpopular, legends of assassination by his own men seem unfounded. It is ironic that the highest-ranking American officer killed was also one of the most detested. Members of the scouting party Ferguson sent out that morning returned as the battle closed, and in the ensuing firefight Williams was probably hit. This detachment escaped, the only Loyalists who were not captured that day.

Glance uphill and note the steep terrain. Firing downhill, the Loyalists were at a disadvantage. Unless trained to correct for it, troops firing downhill will usually overshoot. Colonel Hill wrote that "their shot went over the Americans without effect." Sixteen-year-old Thomas Young recalled that, "Ben Hollingsworth and I took right up the side of the mountain, and fought our way from tree to tree, up to the summit. I recollect I stood behind one tree and fired until the bark was nearly all knocked off. . . ."

A relative of Young, Matthew McCrary, had been taken prisoner by the Loyalists and was forced to fight that day. Unbelievably, Young saw McCrary above him on the ridge. "Matthew discovered me, and ran from the British line, and threw his arms around me for joy." During the action here, Lacy's horse was shot from underneath him, but at the close of the fighting he received Ferguson's black English charger.

Stop 6: The Spring

Continue on the trail until you reach a sharp bend. Stop here and face the hill, note a small spring to your left.

This area of the battlefield illustrates the importance of terrain during the engagement. As you look uphill you can see the ridgeline among the trees, this is even clearer in the fall months. American accounts mention how the Loyalists were silhouetted against the sky, making them easy targets. This point is also one hundred yards from the crest, enabling you to get a visual feel for the effective range of the Loyalist's muskets. As they charged downhill, they will extend their killing zone out. Yet after each bayonet charge, the Loyalists had to return to the hill, which would fatigue the men quickly. At the base of the hill is one of the many springs in the area. This and other sources of water would be used by the wounded of both sides after the fighting closed.

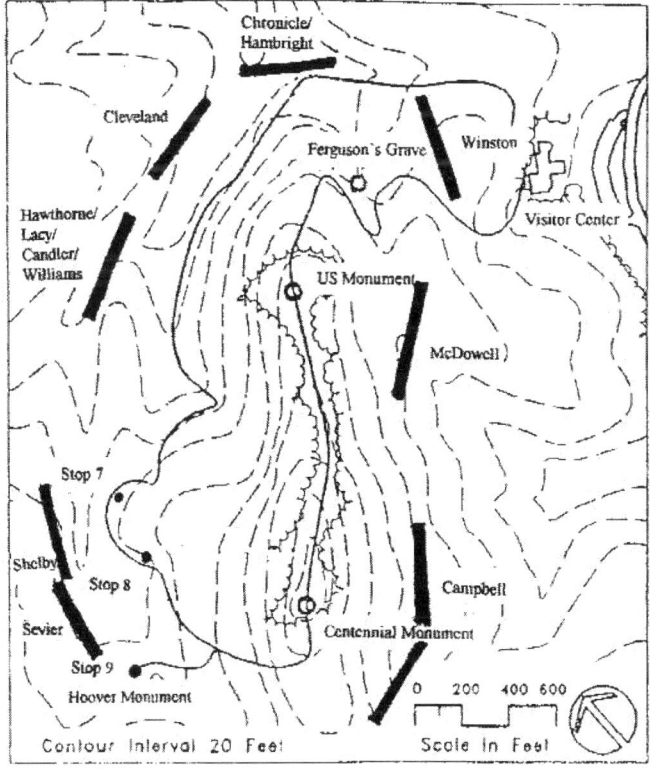

Map 4. Stops 7-9

Stop 7: Shelby's Attack
Proceed until you reach the marker "Be Your Own Officer."

Here fought the Watauga settlers under Colonel Isaac Shelby (Current Sullivan County, TN). These Scotch-Irish settlers led by Shelby and Sevier were tough frontiersmen who until now had remained out of the war raging east of the Blue Ridge Mountains. Many were motivated to come here by Ferguson's threat to lay waste their country, others saw striking out at Ferguson as a way to keep him from reaching their homes. Shelby was the driving force behind organizing the march to meet Ferguson, and his accounts are some of the best describing the battle. Although the Overmountain Men are perhaps the best remembered American troops of the battle, they comprised less than half of the attacking riflemen.

Shelby entered the battle with about one-hundred-twenty men, he lost at least five in the attack. Shelby later wrote, "They repelled us three times with bayonet charges; but being determined to conquer or die, we came up a fourth time." As Shelby's and Sevier's men attacked here, so did Campbell's opposite this position. Of this Shelby recalled, "As either column would approach the summit, Ferguson would order a charge with fixed bayonets, which was always successful, for the riflemen retreated before the charging column slowly, firing as they retired. When Ferguson's men returned to regain their position on the mountain, the patriots would again rally and pursue them." Many accounts mention Shelby's influence on his men, moving among them and rallying the troops after each repulse. Some commanders have the charisma to exert a strong influence on their men; Shelby was among this rare breed.

Stop 8: Sevier's Attack
The next stop is at the other Tennessee Regiment, headed by Sevier. Halt when you reach the marker "Charging Cold Steel."

Attacking up the slope behind you were Colonel John Sevier's Nolichucky troops (this area is currently Washington County, TN). Losses among Sevier's one-hundred-twenty men were about seven.

As Sevier's riflemen advanced from tree to tree, they benefited from the rolling terrain you see to your right. From the point where they left their horses, these men advanced over a series of ridges, which no doubt gave them cover as they neared Kings Mountain. Once reaching this area, however, the flat open slope was ideal for bayonet charges. The slope rising on your left to the crest witnessed several bayonet charges, which drove Sevier's men down to your right.

There remains some question as to where Sevier's troops actually fought. Early maps of the battle place his column on the other side of the ridge, between the commands of Campbell and McDowell. Subsequent research

18

by historians in the twentieth century placed his regiment here. I have followed the National Park Service's official interpretation that Sevier fought here, next to Shelby.

Stop 9: Hoover Monument
Proceed to the Hoover Monument, at the end of a small spur trail.

This marks the spot where President Herbert Hoover's grandstand stood as he dedicated the park in 1930. Joined by the governors of both Carolinas, from here he delivered an address to a crowd estimated at nearly 80,000 people. It was one of the largest gatherings in American history up to that time, occurring in the days before interstates and widespread air travel. Your brochure has a photograph of the crowd, taken from this spot. Note how the facing hillside was cleared for the audience. Secret Service agents kept the public back a respectable distance from the president's grandstand.

By 1930 there was sufficient interest in creating a park at Kings Mountain. Initially the War Department administered the park, as it did other battlefields such as Gettysburg, Chickamauga, and Shiloh. In 1933 the War Department transferred the site to the National Park Service. Kings Mountain was one of the first southern Revolutionary battlefields to become a National Military Park.

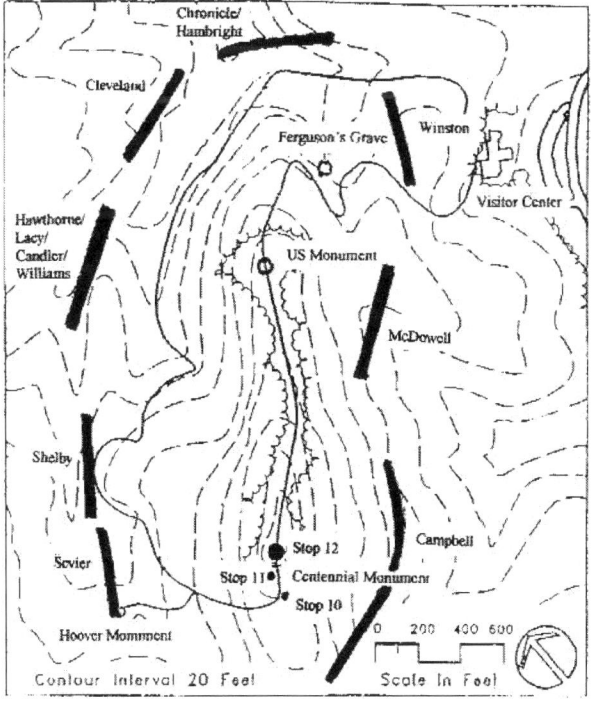

Map 5. Stops 10-12

19

Stop 10: Campbell's Attack
Continue up the trail to the marker "Hammer the Hilltop"

Attacking up the hill towards your position were the Virginians under the command of Colonel William Campbell. Here the battle started, Campbell and the Tennesseans of Sevier and Shelby were the first to engage the Loyalists. Campbell estimates that he was engaged a full ten minutes before the rest of the American troops came into line.

Often overlooked today, the Virginians came the farthest to fight at Kings Mountain, were engaged the longest, had the most men on the field, and suffered the most casualties. Of two hundred men, Campbell's regiment lost thirty-five, many of them officers. One third of the total American losses this day were suffered by the Virginians.

As the Virginians ascended the ridge they were met by a bayonet charge from the Provincial Regulars and driven down the hill. They retreated into the valley and up the hill behind them before stopping. This critical moment of the battle has often been overlooked: a militia panic at the outset of fighting led to the American disaster at Camden just two months earlier. Campbell and his officers were able to rally the men and get them back into the fight. The Virginians made several attempts to storm the ridge, eventually succeeding with the pressure applied by Sevier and Shelby behind you.

Recent archaeology has confirmed that the small rise behind you was also occupied during the fighting. The highest point on the ridge, it may have been held by sharpshooters placed by Ferguson.

Among the Virginians were at least five African-Americans, four of them were free men. Enslaved blacks fought on both sides during the Revolution, taking advantage of offers of freedom made by the English and Americans. Slave owners could also avoid the draft by using slaves as a substitute. Many free blacks also served in both armies, having as much at stake in the outcome as white colonists.

The Loyalist bayonet charges here inflicted many casualties. Ensign Robert Campbell wrote that his men "obsintately stood until some of them were thrust through the body, and having nothing but their rifles by which to defend themselves, were forced to retreat." Remember at close quarters riflemen are helpless when facing bayonets.

Drury Mathis, a Loyalist who lived on the Broad River, fell wounded in the third bayonet charge. He hugged the ground playing dead, watching the Virginians charge around him up the hillside. The next day he was taken to a nearby home and nursed back to health. Mathis eventually rejoined the British at Ninety Six.

The Edmonson family of Virginia claims the honor of having the most relatives at Kings Mountain: seven Edmonsons fought here, including three lieutenants, one captain, and one major. Two were killed, and one became wounded.

Eventually the Virginians gained the crest here, as did the units of Shelby and Sevier attacking the other side of the ridge. From here the Americans pushed the Loyalists down the length of the hill. As you proceed along the trail you will be following that retrograde movement.

Stop 11: The Provincial Regulars
Just up from the marker for Campbell's men stands one for the Provincials, "Americans in Redcoats."

Most of Ferguson's army were local militia wearing their civilian clothing. Ferguson did have a one hundred man detachment known as the American Volunteers. These troops were Provincial Regulars: Americans who had formally enlisted into the British army. Provincial Regiments were numbered like other English line regiments, received British pay, wore red coats, and after the war were eligible for land grants and pensions just like English troops.

The American Volunteers were made up of troops from four regiments raised in the New York City area: the Kings American Regiment, the Loyal American Regiment, the Prince of Wales Regiment and the New Jersey Volunteers. These soldiers hailed from New York, New Jersey, and Connecticut. They had traveled south to participate in the siege of Charleston and joined Ferguson later that summer. They were also the best men Ferguson had and used them as shock troops wherever needed.

The Provincials met Campbell's Virginians with fierce bayonet charges. Dr. Uzal Johnson, a surgeon with the Loyalists, recalled that "As soon as they got to the Brow of the Hill, the American Volunteers charged them with success and drove them down the Hill, but were not able to pursue, our number being too small. We then retreated in order to gain the height and prevent their getting possession of it."

As they repulsed Campbell's men they then turned to face Shelby and Sevier. In this fashion they alternated counterattacks in the first part of the battle. The American Volunteers were then sent down the length of the ridge to strengthen that sector near the modern US Monument.

Losses among the Provincials were dreadful: about fifty-three were killed or wounded of this small detachment. Many of the Provincials who were captured escaped and returned to British service by the end of the war. Their presence here in red coats has led to two long-standing myths about Kings Mountain. First, that Ferguson's men were English regulars, and secondly that the Loyalists were all wearing red coats.

Stop 12: Centennial Monument
Proceed up the ridge to the Centennial Monument, the highest point on the trail.

Here, on this prominent rise, descendants of the American army placed this monument in 1880. The one hundredth anniversary of the battle was celebrated in grand style with parades, patriotic music, fireworks, and picnics.

The anniversary also fostered interest in preserving the battlefield, and the Kings Mountain Centennial Association, who had organized the event, bought 39.5 acres consisting of the length of the ridge. Adjoining lands were bought in the 1930s by the Federal Government. This is the highest point along the trail (1019'), although Brown's Mountain is the highest point in the park (1045'). The elevation of other points are listed below:

Visitor Center: 850'

US Monument: 960'

As you proceed down the trail look closely at the terrain on each side of the slope. The military makes a distinction between the topographical crest and the military crest which is important to note here. The trail follows the topographical crest: the highest point along the ridgeline. Here troops are too far back from the edge and would not see approaching soldiers. Ferguson's men would have held the military crest, closer to the edge, well off the trail, to see down hill and make their charges. As you move on pause periodically to appreciate the Loyalist view, now that you have seen the American perspective from below.

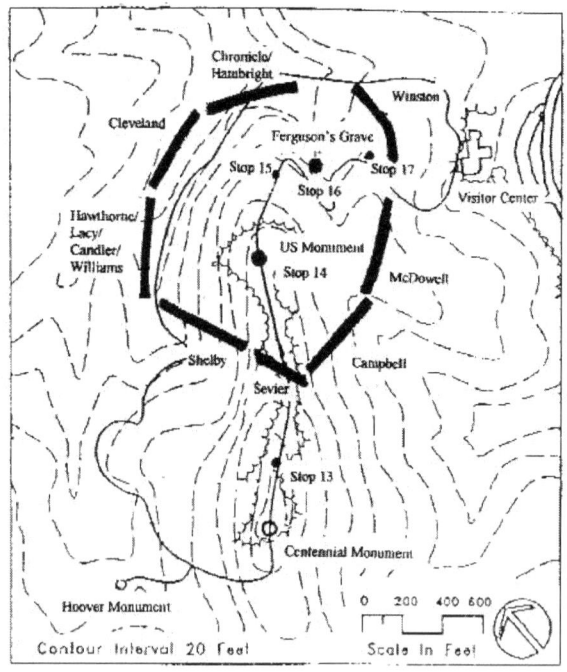

Map 6. Stops 13-17

22

Stop 13: Loyalist Militia
Continue to the marker entitled "Loyal Carolina Men."

The bulk of Ferguson's army consisted of local Loyalist militia. Raised in both Carolinas, these troops had drilled under Ferguson's watchful eye all summer. They were equipped with muskets and bayonets, but probably had a few scattered rifles among them. They had been instructed in the traditional drill of the British army, which stressed volley fire and use of the bayonet. Men who did not have socket bayonets were given plug bayonets: knives with the wooden handles whittled down to fit into the muzzle. None had uniforms.

As the English took over much of South Carolina that summer, they established a militia system to guard the forts and posts across the state and maintain order. This illustrated the level of Loyalism in the state, and how far the English had come in reestablishing their authority here. Ferguson had parts of six militia regiments with him at Kings Mountain: the Little River Militia, the Dutch Fork Regiment, the Stevens Creek Militia, the Spartan Regiment, Fair Forest Militia, and Long Cane Militia. We do not know much about how these troops were broken down into companies or detachments, or where specifically each unit was located on the ridge.

Even amid the death and suffering, humorous incidents occurred. Samuel Abney, a South Carolinian held as a prisoner by the Loyalists, was hit when the battle started, making him "a little mad." When he was hit a second time, he became "mighty mad," and picked up a musket to join the Loyalists in defending the ridge. He ended up with seven wounds and was left unconscious. Local citizens found him and nursed him back to health.

Lieutenant Alexander Chesney, a local Loyalist who lived near Cowpens and commanded a small detachment here recorded the battle in his diary. He wrote that the Americans "took post and opened an irregular but destructive fire from behind trees and other cover. The mountaineers, flying from when in danger from a bayonet charge, and returned as soon as the British faced about to repel another of their party."

The Loyalists had been drilled in traditional open-field tactics, which stressed volley fire and bayonet charges. Their counterattacks would have worked against the Americans in most places, except the wooded hillsides of Kings Mountain. With each bayonet charge, the American riflemen retreated, but they could find cover and reload in the forest. The woods also negated the effectiveness of Loyalist musket volleys.

The battle at Kings Mountain would be the high water mark for these Upcountry Carolina Loyalists. With the American militia and Continental army on the run, they held sway over wide regions of South Carolina after years of American rule. Never again would they exercise so much control or be a serious threat to American forces after this day.

Face to the west (your left as you look downhill to the US Monument)

Attacking the Loyalists up this slope were the South Carolinians under Lacy and Williams, as well as Cleveland's North Carolina regiment. From here you can appreciate the Loyalist view of their attack.

Face to the east (your right as you look downhill toward the US Monument)

Attacking toward your position from the east were Major Joseph McDowell's Burke and Rutherford County militia, ninety men strong. Some of his troops hailed from the South Carolina upcountry as well. Their approach up the hill was fairly gentle compared to that of other detachments. As you walk the crest bear in mind that one line of Loyalist troops faced downhill to your right, the other stood on your left. Towards the close of the battle, these men were caught in a crossfire. McDowell lost at least ten men in the attack.

The Robertson brothers of Rutherford County, William and Thomas, were among McDowell's column. One of their neighbors fighting with the Loyalists named Lafferty, recognized them and called out to Thomas, who peered out from behind his tree. Lafferty's shot missed, but Thomas's reply did not. This is just one example of neighbors meeting each other across the firing line.

Stop 14: the US Monument

Your next stop is at the US Monument, standing in the large open clearing.

Placed here by Congress in 1909, this monument has become known as the US Monument. It marks the site of the Loyalist camp, where tents, wagons, and baggage were set up. Ferguson's marquee was somewhere in this clearing. This field was also open in 1780, the soil being too rocky for tree roots. Here the battle ended and the Loyalists began to surrender.

As they were pushed down the hill from the direction of the Centennial Monument, confusion and panic spread in the Loyalist ranks. Surrounded, caught in a crossfire, and low on ammunition, some began to surrender. The linear formations upon which they needed to function had been disrupted. Units were intermingled, and officers hit. Ferguson tore down several white flags, and many Americans refused to honor them anyway. The riflemen had the recent massacre at the Waxhaws on their mind and kept firing until officers gained control of them. Amid the noise, smoke, and confusion, it was difficult to maintain order. Eventually the Loyalists were allowed to lay down their arms. It was all over in about an hour.

Here is the account of John Long, a Tennessean who observed the close of the fighting: "I know that Colonel Shelby went bravely into the action, and that it was his influence that rallied our troops . . . I saw him at the surrender, and know that he first stopped the firing on the enemy, declaring that as they surrendered, they ought not to be fired on, which some were disposed to do, who were crying out 'Buford's play.'"

Fighting on both sides were several friends, neighbors, and family members. Two Logan brothers of Lincoln County, NC fought for Ferguson, two with the Americans. All lived peacefully with their neighbors after the war. The GoForths of Cleveland County, NC, had three brothers on the Loyalist side and two with the Americans. The war in the South was very personal: splitting friends, households, and communities.

The morning of the battle Ferguson sent out a scouting party of about two hundred men. They returned as the battle was closing to find the Americans in possession of the hill and their comrades broken. A brief firefight ensued, in which the detachment was driven off. Colonel Campbell relates that a number of Loyalist prisoners here in the clearing were cut down in the crossfire.

Loyalist doctor Uzal Johnson treated the wounded of both sides in the aftermath. The only surgeon present and lacking appropriate medical supplies, the work must have been overwhelming.

Stop 15: Ferguson Fell Marker
Continue to the marker for Ferguson's wounding at the lower end of the ridge.

Realizing the situation was hopeless, Ferguson attempted to cut his way out on horseback. In this vicinity he was hit simultaneously by several riflemen. His foot caught in the stirrup, and the horse dragged him downhill.

Downhill to your left is a marker for Hambright, wounded in the thigh as he led the South Fork Troops up the hill towards you. After the war Hambright owned land nearby, and died in a log house about a mile away in 1817 at the age of 90. Many of the men who claimed to have shot Ferguson were from Sevier's regiment, which would have been on the other side of the mountain. Perhaps, as troops became intermingled in the confusion, some of the Tennesseans worked their way over to this area.

Stop 16: Ferguson's Grave
Proceed down the hill to Ferguson's Cairn.

Placed here in 1930, this cairn is a traditional Scottish burial. According to accounts, Ferguson's men buried him in a cowhide at the base of the hill. The only Briton in the battle, the young officer's loss was a severe blow to the English army. American troops and officers freely took souvenirs such as Ferguson's sword, pistols, sash, watch, and other belongings. Today they are on display in the Tennessee State Museum in Nashville.

Private James Collins of South Carolina witnessed Ferguson's burial. He wrote, "on examining the dead body of their great chief, it appeared that about fifty rifles must have been leveled at him, at the same time: Seven rifle balls had passed through his body, both of his arms were broken, and his hat and clothing were literally shot to pieces."

A long-standing myth has been that the American riflemen gathered around Ferguson's lifeless body and urinated on him. Earlier Ferguson had proclaimed that unless the Americans wished to be pissed upon they should look for real men to protect him. While a popular story, there is little evidence that his body was defiled.

One of those who buried Ferguson was Loyalist Elias Powell of Caldwell County, NC. Powell managed to salvage his commander's silver whistles. Powell returned to his home, and died in 1832, a well respected member of the community.

Ferguson had two servants with him during the battle: Virginia Sal and Virginia Paul. British army regulations allowed women to serve with regiments in the field as cooks, nurses, and laundresses. They received pay and half rations. Sal was killed and buried with Ferguson. Virginia Paul was taken as a prisoner to Salem, and later turned over to the British army.

Recent archaeological testing has confirmed that Ferguson and Sal are here. Ground penetrating radar, similar to an x-ray machine, has produced an image showing two anomalies under the ground.

Stop 17: Americans Victorious/American Vanquished
Move up the hill to the markers explaining the close of the battle.

The Americans lost just ninety-two men:, while the Loyalists suffered nearly four hundred casualties (225 killed, 123 wounded, total: 345, and 716 captured). Except for a small group sent out that morning, Ferguson's entire army was killed, wounded, or captured. In one hour the English had lost one third of their manpower in South Carolina. Along with their prisoners, the Americans also captured 1,500 arms, 17 wagons, powder, lead, cattle, and horses.

Physically all were exhausted: the Loyalists from bayonet charges and the Americans from their overnight march and uphill attacks. Thomas Young wrote that during the battle he fired two balls from his musket. "The recoil was dreadful, but I had not noticed it in the action." No doubt as adrenaline subsided the men of both sides were overcome with fatigue.

Both armies had to camp, as Virginia soldier Benjamin Sharp recalled, "with the dead and wounded, and pass the night amid groans and lamentations." The Americans had traveled light and did not have much food with them. Neither did Ferguson's army. The evening wind can whip fiercely up the steep slopes, and no doubt both groups spent a cold, hungry night on the mountain.

The next morning private James Collins recalled that "the wives and children of the poor Tories came in, in great numbers. Their husbands, fathers, and brothers, lay in heaps, while others lay wounded or dying . . . We proceeded to bury the dead, but it was badly done; they were thrown into convenient piles, and covered with old logs, the bark of old trees, and rocks; yet not so as to secure them from becoming prey to the beasts of the forest, or the vultures of the air; and the wolves became so plenty, that it was dangerous for any one to be out at night, for several miles around. . . ."

The dead were apparently buried in three mass graves, one American and two for the Loyalists. Their location remains unknown to this day. With continuing research, the park staff does hope to locate and properly mark these sites.

The next morning Campbell left a small detachment to bury the dead, while the rest of the army moved out. The Americans feared Colonel Banistre Tarelton's dragoons would move out from Charlotte to intercept them. By nightfall of the 8th they had reunited with the slower detachment coming from Cowpens.

The Americans marched north, taking their prisoners with them. With eight hundred men guarding about seven hundred, there were nearly as many prisoners as guards, and the Loyalists were forced to carry their own muskets, with flints removed. At Bickerstaff's plantation, near Rutherfordton, North Carolina, tempers boiled over. Among the prisoners were men known to have committed murder and plundering that summer.

A trial was hastily convened, and thirty Loyalists were condemned to hang. Many of the Americans were extracting revenge against the Tories for earlier atrocities. Nine men were hung before Shelby, Campbell, and the other officers put a stop to the hangings. The war in the South had become a cycle of violence and revenge.

As the Americans moved north various detachments broke off to return home. The prisoners were conducted to the Moravain towns near Salem, North Carolina. Ironically, most escaped, and fought again with the British at Ninety Six the following summer.

Aftermath

The significance of Kings Mountain lies in its timing. 1780 had been a bleak year for the Americans: Benedict Arnold defected to the British, Washington's troops mutinied at Morristown, NJ, and the English invasion of the South seemed unstoppable. After a string of devastating defeats (Savannah, Charleston, Camden, Fishing Creek, Waxhaw) the Americans had finally won a decisive victory. In one hour the entire enemy force was killed, wounded, or captured: few battles in American history are so complete. More importantly, the English plan to use Loyalist to crush the rebellion was ruined. Never again could the British army count on Loyalist support as they marched through the Carolinas. The dead men buried at Kings Mountain and Bickerstaff's plantation showed the price for loyalty to the crown.

The day after the battle Colonel John Sevier wrote that, "The tide will turn from this hour forward in favor of the Americans." He was right. With a sizable part of his army destroyed, Cornwallis retreated from Charlotte to Winnsboro, SC, delaying his invasion of North Carolina until spring. This granted the Continental army a much needed chance to rest and reorganize. Newly arrived from the north, General Nathaniel Greene prepared to take the initiative.

The English never won another battle in the South: they met defeat three months later at Cowpens, and drove Greene's army off at Guilford Courthouse in March but suffered atrocious losses. Nearly one year later, on October 19, 1781, Cornwallis surrendered his battered army at Yorktown, Virginia. General Henry Clinton, British commander in North America, called Kings Mountain "the first link in a chain of evils, that resulted in the total loss of America."

From Battleground to Park

The 1780 engagement was fought in a climax forest among old growth trees. This area was the frontier, there were few roads or towns in the region. Within a few decades, settlement began to open up the area. The forest of Kings Mountain has been cleared several times, most recently in 1930. Many old photos and sketches from the nineteenth and early twentieth century attest to the cleared hillsides here.

In 1815 patriotism swept the nation as a result of the War of 1812. Dr. William McLean of Gaston County North Carolina, a Congressional candidate, came to dedicate the Chronicle Marker. At least seven of the South Fork troops were present in 1815, just thirty-five years after the battle. McLean felt the battlefield should not be neglected, and placed the Chronicle Marker to that end. He also gathered the scattered remains of the dead and buried them properly. This unmarked grave has not been located, but archaeology has concluded that there are no burials at the Chronicle Marker.

By 1855 the region was thriving with the prosperity of the antebellum years. In the nearby town of Yorkville, Asbury Coward formed the Kings Mountain Military Academy. His cadets came to the battlefield annually to drill. The Civil War saw the demise of his school, but after the war Coward took an avid interest in preserving this site.

In 1880 local citizens headed by Coward formed the Kings Mountain Centennial Association to organize a ceremony on the battle's one hundredth anniversary. The Association purchased from the landowners 39.5 acres, consisting of the battlefield ridge between the Centennial and Chronicle markers. During a three day celebration that October, several thousands visited the site. Bands played patriotic music, while barbecues, fireworks, parades, and a mock reenactment completed the festivities. At the close of the ceremony the Centennial Monument was unveiled.

Within a few years a local chapter of the Daughters of the American Revolution from Yorkville purchased the tract of land. They encouraged the Federal Government to recognize the site, resulting in the dedication of the US Monument in 1909.

By 1930 Congress agreed to create a National Military Park at the site, and President Herbert Hoover came to officially dedicate the park. The War Department initially administered the site, until it was transferred to the National Park Service in 1933. These were lean years during the Great Depression, but the park benefited from work by the Civilian Conservation Corps.

The CCC built roads, bridges, and structures in the park. The state park's Lake Crawford, road system, bathhouse, and the national park headquarters are examples of CCC architecture and work projects. In 1940 the park was split into a recreation area, given to the state, and the battlefield. The current visitor center was built in 1975, a project of the Bicentennial.

As explained in the Introduction, Kings Mountain is a unique Revolutionary War site. Fought in the woods, with rifles and muskets, and by Americans on both sides, it is not a typical Revolutionary battle and has not been seen that way in popular culture. Many books, films, and legends place Kings Mountain in the same category with the Alamo, New Orleans, Horseshoe Bend, or Point Pleasant. It was a battle fought on the frontier, by frontiersmen. It holds the attraction of longhunters and pioneers defending their liberty, although the real story is much more complicated than that.

Controversies

Interestingly, the battle has many controversies, some of which historians still debate. The death of Colonel James Williams has always been considered suspicious, yet proof that he was targeted by his own men remains skeptical. One account even states that Ferguson himself shot Williams as he was dying. As related above, the position of Sevier's troops on the ridge has also been contested.

As hard as it is to believe, the presence of Patrick Ferguson's own rifles here remains in doubt. While there is no conclusive evidence either way, it seems likely that at least some were present, perhaps among officers or sharpshooters. Ferguson probably would have wanted his rifles when he came south for his new command. Yet no American accounts mention capturing this unique weapon, while nearly every other type of accoutrement taken is noted. Perhaps future research and archaeology will settle the issue.

One of the most heated controversies arose in the 1820s about Colonel William Campbell's role in the battle. Many officers from other units felt that Campbell hung back out of danger while the battle raged. Apparently Campbell and his servant John Broddy resembled each other from a distance,

30

and it was Broddy that people confused with Campbell. Relatives of the commander cleared his name after heated debate. Finally, the death of Patrick Ferguson is also debated, as one account claims he was killed at the outset of the battle, while others state he died at the end. These unresolved issues illustrate how little firsthand information we have about this famous battle.

Park Monuments

Several monuments stand in the park, ranging from small plaques to impressive memorials. Unlike monuments at Civil War sites that were placed by the veterans, these monuments were dedicated by later descendants of the Kings Mountain soldiers. The history of each is outlined below.

Chronicle Markers (3)

There are three monuments to William Chronicle, who fell at the head of the South Fork Troops. The first, placed in 1815, is one of the oldest Revolutionary War monuments in the nation. It has been badly weathered over the years. This marker was replaced in 1915 with a newer stone, copying the same inscription. Both monuments read:

> Sacred to the memory of Maj. William Chronicle, Capt. John Mattocks, William Rabb, and John Boyd, who were killed at this place on the 7th of October, 1780, fighting in defense of America.

The reverse says:

> Colonel Ferguson, an officer of His Britannic Majesty, was defeated and killed at this place on the 7th of October, 1780.

In 1925 another maker was placed a few yards uphill to honor Chronicle.

Coward Marker

This plaque recognizes Colonel Asbury Coward, a resident of York who was instrumental in establishing the park. Coward served as a colonel in the 5th South Carolina during the Civil War, and had opened a military academy at York before the war. His cadets came to the battleground to drill annually. After the war Coward, with the support of the Daughters of the American Revolution, helped foster interest in a park at Kings Mountain. This tablet was placed here in 1931. It originally stood closer to the Centennial Monument.

Hawthorne Marker

In the shadow of the US Monument stands this marker to Col. James Hawthorne, a somewhat forgotten leader. Hawthorne assisted in directing the South Carolina Troops in the battle. This tablet was placed in 1949.

Kings Mountain Marker

Originally located on the battlefield, this marker was erected in 1931. It now stands along the road at the eastern entrance to the park, bordering the state park.

Ferguson Fell Marker

Approximating the site where Ferguson was struck from his horse, this stone was placed here in 1909. It is inscribed, "Here Ferguson Fell Oct. 7, 1780."

Hambright Marker

Downhill from the site of Ferguson's wounding, Frederick Hambright was hit directing the South Fork men. Hambright lived nearby after the war and many descendants live in the region today. This monument was placed here in 1939.

Ferguson's Carin

The monument and cairn (rock pile) date to 1931. Here Patrick Ferguson and Virginia Sal are buried. A cairn is a traditional Scottish burial. The inscription reveals how ties between England and the United States grew during the early twentieth century.

Hoover Marker

This simple stone and bronze plaque marks the site of Hoover's grandstand during the park's dedication ceremony. From here the president addressed a crowd estimated at nearly 80,000. The stone was placed here in 1931.

Centennial Monument

Dedicated during the 1880 celebration, this monument stands at the highest point along the trail. The marker honors the American officers and several of the Virginia troops who fell in the battle. It reads:

In Memory of
the Patriotic Americans
who participated in the
Battle of Kings Mountain
This monument is erected
by their grateful
Descendants

Fell on this battleground in
Defense of Civil Liberty
Col. James Williams
Maj. William Chronicle
—Captains—
John Mattocks, David Beatie
—First Lieutenants—
Reece Bowen, Thomas McCullough
William Blackburn, Robert Edmonston
—Second Lieutenants—
John Beattie, Andrew Edmonson
Humberson Lyon, James Corry
James Laird, Nathaniel Guist
Nathaniel Dryden, James Phillips
—Privates—
William Rabb, John Boyd, David Duff
Henry Heniger, William Watson
Arthur Patterson, Preston GoForth

Here on the 7th day of
October A.D. 1780
The British forces
commanded by
Col. PATRICK FERGUSON
were met and totally defeated by
CAMPBELL, SHELBY,
WILLIAMS, CLEVELAND,
SEVIER, and their followers
from Virginia, the Carolinas,
and Tennessee

Here the tide of Battle
turned in favor of the
AMERICAN COLONIES

US Monument

Placed by the federal government in 1909, the US Monument was designed by the prestigious New York firm of McKim, Mead, and White. The obelisk stands on the site of Ferguson's camp, and the area of the Loyalist surrender. Its inscription reads:

To commemorate the victory of Kings Mountain
October 7, 1780

By the Government of the United States
To the establishment of which the heroism and patriotism of
those who participated in this battle so largely contributed.

On this field the Patriot forces attacked and defeated an equal force of Tories and British Regular Troops. The British commander, Major Patrick Ferguson, was killed, and his entire force was captured after suffering heavy losses. This brilliant victory marked the turning point of the American Revolution.

Killed

Col. James Williams	Private Thomas Bicknell
Lt. Col. James Steen	John Boyd
Capt. William Edmonson	John Brown
Maj. William Chronicle	David Duff
Capt. John Mattocks	Preston GoForth
First Lt. William Blackburn	Henry Henigar
Reece Bowen	Michael Mahoney
Robert Edmonson, Sr.	Arthur Patterson
Second Lt. John Beattle	William Ruff
James Corry	John Smart
Nathaniel Gist	Daniel Siske
Humberson Lyon	William Steele
James Phillips	William Watson
	Unknown

Mortally Wounded

Capt. John Sevier Second	Lt. James Laird
First Lt. Thomas McCullough	Private Moss Henry

Wounded

Lt. Col. Frederick Hambright
Maj. Michael Lewis
James Poter
Capt. James Dysart
William Lenoir
Samuel Espy
Joel Lewis
Moses Shelby
Minor Smith
First Lt. Robert Edmonson, Jr.
Samuel Gordon
Samuel Johnson
Samuel Newell
JM Smith
Private Benoni Banning
William Bradley
William Bullen
John Childress

Private John Chittim
William Cox
John Fagan
Frederick Fisher
William Giles
_____ Gilleland
William Gilmer
Israel Hayter
Robert Henry
Leonard Hyce
Charles Kilgore
Robert Miller
William Moore
Patrick Murphy
William Robertson
John Skeggs
24 Unknown Wounded

Commanders

Washington Co. (VA)	Col. William Campbell
Washington Co. NC (now TN)	Col. John Sevier
Sullivan Co. NC (now TN)	Col. Isaac Shelby
Ninety Six District, SC; Rowan Co., NC	Col. James Williams
Wilkes and Surry Co., NC	Col. Benjamin Cleveland
	Maj. Joseph Winston
Burke and Rutherford Co., NC	Maj. Joseph McDowell
Lincoln Co., NC	Lt. Col. Frederick Hambright
	Col. William Chronicle
York, Chester Co., SC	
(Part of Camden District, SC	Col. Edward Lacy
	Col. William Hill
Georgia	Maj. William Candler

Reserves

Col. James Johnston

Note. Col. Charles McDowell, the regular commander of the Burke and Rutherford County Regiment, was absent from the battle on a special mission to General Gates.

British Forces

Maj. Patrick Ferguson (K)   Captain Abraham DePeyster

Orders of Battle

American Forces
Colonel William Campbell
Campbell (Virginia Militia–200)
Col. John Sevier (North Carolina Militia–120)
Col. Isaac Shelby (North Carolina Militia–120)
Maj. Joseph Winston (Surry County Militia–60)
Maj. Joseph McDowell (Burke and Rutherford Co. Militia–90)
Col. William Chronicle (South Fork Militia–20)
Maj. Benjamin Cleveland (Surry County Militia–110)
Cols. Edward Lacey, and James Hawthorne (South Carolina Militia)
Col. James Williams (South Carolina Militia) SC Total: 70
Col. William Candler (Georgia Militia–30)

US Total: 910
Casualties: 92

Loyalist Forces
Major Patrick Ferguson
Lt. Col. Abraham DePeyster

Lt. Anthony Allaire–American Volunteers (120)
Maj. David Plummer–Fair Forest Militia (160)
Maj. Patrick Cunningham–Little River Militia (230)
Dutch Fork Militia (10)*
Long Cane Militia (40)*
Stevens Creek Militia (100)*
Spartan Militia (140)*
Tryon County, NC Militia (?)*

Loyalist Total: 1100
Casualties: 900 (killed, wounded, captured)

The commanders of most of these regiments is unknown, as is their exact strength

Loyalists executed at Bickerstaff's plantation

Colonel Ambrose Mills
Lieutenant Lafferty
Captain Walter Gilkey
Captain James Chitwood
Captain Grimes
Captain Robert Wilson
John McFall
John Bibby
Augustine Hobbs

These are the loyalists hung at Bickerstaffs by the American army. While no doubt some of these men did commit atrocities, they were hung without benefit of fair trial.

Nearby Sites

George Washington was one of the nation's first battlefield tourists. He enjoyed visiting the sites of Revolutionary battles and saw many during his presidential visit to South Carolina in 1791. While in the area consider visiting these nearby sites related to the Kings Mountain Campaign. These are all within a few hours of Kings Mountain:

Buford Battleground. Site of the Battle of the Waxahws. This American defeat, in which Col. Banister Tarleton slaughtered American prisoners, inspired the American militia to fight at Kings Mountain.

Charlotte Museum of History. Preserves the Alexander home, the oldest house in Mecklenburg County. Museum exhibits tell of Charlotte during the Revolution.

Cowpens National Battlefield. Campsite for the American army and site of another decisive battle three months later. McDowell's militia served here as well.

Guilford Courthouse National Military Park. Climactic battle site of the southern campaign, fought five months after Kings Mountain. Militia under Campbell and Winston fought here as well.

Historic Brattonsville. Living history farm and site of a prior skirmish involving Hill and Lacy's troops. Parts of the recent film *The Patriot* were filmed here.

Museum of the Waxhaws. Exhibits discuss the settlement of the region and Revolutionary War battles fought in the area.

Musgrove Mill State Historic Park. The American Volunteers under DePeyster met defeat at the hands of Shelby, Williams, and other leaders. This battle occurred just one month before Kings Mountain.

Ninety Six National Historic Site. This park preserves the site of two Revolutionary war battles, including the longest siege of the entire war. Ninety Six was the center of activity for this region, with a jail, courthouse, and trading post. From here Ferguson set out for North Carolina. Many Loyalists who fought at Kings Mountain escaped to this British post.

Williams's Grave. Buried in front of the old library in downtown Gaffney lies Colonel James Williams, killed in the battle of Kings Mountain. The site is just ten miles from the park.

Hambright's Grave. Lieutenant Colonel Frederick Hambright is buried just a few miles from the park near I-85. Hambright owned land near the battlefield and lived there until the age of 90. Ask at the information desk for directions to his grave.

These sites, located across the Carolinas and Virginia, tell the larger story of the Southern Campaign:

Colonial National Historic Park. After failing to subdue the Carolinas Cornwallis moved into Virginia. Yorktown battlefield preserves the site of Cornwallis's surrender to General Washington in 1781. It was the last major battle of the war, and broke English enthusiasm for its continuance.

Fort Moultrie National Monument. Site of a failed British attempt to take Charleston in 1776. The defense of the fort is commemorated in South Carolina's state flag.

Historic Camden Revolutionary War Site. Earthworks and structures preserve the site of the British army's encampment. Nearby are markers for two battles fought at Camden.

Moores Creek National Battlefield. This American victory early in the war left the rebels in firm control of the south, but left many Loyalists with a burning desire for revenge.

Andrew Jackson State Park. Birthplace of the future seventh president. As a teenager Jackson fought in the American militia, was wounded, and held as a British prisoner. Exhibits tell the story of the Revolution in the area.

Web sites

These Web sites offer more information about the Revolution and Kings Mountain:

www.nps.gov/kimo: the park's official Web site, with information on special events

www.nps.gov/revwar: National Park Service Revolutionary War Web site

www.nps.gov/ovvi: information on the Overmountain Victory Trial, commemorating the American march to the battle

www.ovta.org: The group which retraces the march of the mountain men every October

Recommended Reading

Alden, John. *The South in the Revolution.* Baton Rouge: Louisiana State University Press, 1976.

Alderman, Pat. *The Overmountain Men.* Johnson City, TN: Overmountain Press, 1986.

Bailey, JD. *Commanders at Kings Mountain.* Greenville, SC: A Press Inc., 1992.

Buchanan, John C. *The Road to Guilford Courthouse.* New York: Wiley Sons, 1997.

Draper, Lyman C. *Kings Mountain and Its Heroes.* Johnson City, TN: Overmountain Press, 1996.

Lumpkin, Henry. *From Savannah to Yorktown.* Columbia: University of South Carolina Press, 1981.

Morrill, Dan. *The Southern Campaigns of the American Revolution.* Mt Pleasant, SC: Nautical and Aviation Publishers, 1993.

Moss, Bobby, ed. *Uzal Johnson: Loyalist Surgeon.* Blacksburg, SC: Scotia Hibernia Press, 2000.

Russell, David Lee. *The American Revolution in the Southern Colonies.* Jefferson, NC: McFarland and Company, 2000.

Unfortunately, not much has been written about the battle of Kings Mountain. The best study of the engagement remains Draper's work. Many of the others listed above are good sources on the southern campaign. With the recent growth of interest in the Revolution it is hoped that Kings Mountain will be given the detailed study it deserves.

Bibliography

Addison, Stephen O. *Profile of a Patriot.* Cleveland, TN, 1993.

Bailey, JD. *Commanders at Kings Mountain.* Greenville, SC: A Press Inc., 1992.

Bearss, Edwin C. *Historic Resource Study: Roads, Trails, and Burial Sites, Kings Mountain National Military Park.* Denver: National Park Service, 1974.

Blythe, Robert, Maureen Carroll, and Steven Moffson. *Kings Mountain National Military Park: Historic Resource Study.* Atlanta: National Park Service, 1995.

Buchanan, John C. *The Road to Guilford Courthouse.* New York: Wiley Sons, 1997.

Draper, Lyman C. *Kings Mountain and Its Heroes.* Johnson City, TN: Overmountain Press, 1996.

Graves, William. *James Williams.* Lincoln, NE: Iuniverse, 2002.

Halchin, Jill. *Trip Report on Ground Penetrating Radar Survey, Kings Mountain National Military Park.* Unpublished report on file at Kings Mountain NMP, 2002.

Historical Statements Concerning the Battle of Kings Mountain and the Battle of Cowpens. Washington, DC: Government Printing Office, 1928.

Messick, Hank. *Kings Mountain.* Boston: Little, Brown, and Co., 1976.

Moore, M.A. *Life of Generaly Edward Lacy.* Greenville, SC: A Press Inc., 1981.

Moss, Bobby. *Loyalists at Kings Mountain.* Blacksburg, SC: Scotia Hibernia Press, 1998.

Moss, Bobby. *Patriots at Kings Mountain.* Blacksburg, SC: Scotia Hibernia Press, 1990.

Moss, Bobby, ed. *Uzal Johnson: Loyalist Surgeon.* Blacksburg, SC: Scotia Hibernia Press, 2000.

Roberts, John, ed. *Autobiography of a Revolutionary War Soldier.* North Stratford, NH: Ayer Company Publishing, 1989.

Salley, A.S. *Colonel William Hill's Memoirs.* Columbia: Historical Commission of South Carolina, 1921.